BIG, SCARY ANIMALS

Matt Lyle

BROADWAY PLAY PUBLISHING INC
New York
www.broadwayplaypub.com
info@broadwayplaypub.com

BIG, SCARY ANIMALS
© Copyright 2018 Matt Lyle

Cover art by Kim Rae Lyle

First edition: May 2018
I S B N: 978-0-88145-778-0

Book design: Marie Donovan
Page make-up: Adobe InDesign
Typeface: Palatino

BIG, SCARY ANIMALS was first produced as
CEDAR SPRINGS OR BIG, SCARY ANIMALS from
7 September–1 October 2017 by Theatre Three, Dallas
(Artistic Director, Jeffrey Schmidt; Managing Director,
Merri Brewer; Company Manager, Sarah Barnes). The
cast and creative contributors were:

DONALD .... John S Davies
RHONDA .... Charlotte Akin
MARCUS.. Wilbur Penn
CLARK...Chad Cline
SOPHIA.. Alle Mims
RONNIE .... Jaxon Beeson

Director.. Jeffrey Schmidt
Assistant director....................................Richard T Quadri
Set design ....David Walsh
Costume design...Ryan D Schaap
Lighting design ....Bryant Yeager
Stage manager.. Kevin Keating
Production assistant ....Connor John

ACKNOWLEDGMENTS

Thanks and love to the following: Kim Lyle, Jeffrey Schmidt, Matt Coleman, Kelli Bland, Tina Parker, Chris Carlos, Lee Trull, Kevin Moriarty, David and Connie Lyle, Michael Cooper, and Chris Polson.

CHARACTERS & SETTING

DONALD, *White, married to* CONNIE, *50s–60s, male*
RHONDA, *White, married to* DONALD, *50s–60s, female*
MARCUS, *African-American, married to* CLARK, *40–50s, male*
CLARK, *White, married to* MARCUS, *40s, male*
SOPHIA, *African-American,* MARCUS *and* CLARK's *daughter, 19-20, female*
RONNIE, *White,* DONALD *and* RHONDA's *son, 18*

Time: A simpler time—the Fall of 2015

AUTHOR'S NOTES

On location— The neighborhood which is referenced in the script, Cedar Springs, is the actual "gay neighborhood" in Dallas, TX where the play was first produced. If you'd like, you may adapt that for your city if you'd like a more local feel. Just replace the name of the neighborhood and the street referenced. Same for Donald and Rhonda's hometown. In the script they're from just outside of Paris, Texas. Most states have a Paris... If yours doesn't, you may adjust accordingly and drop Clark's French joke.

DEDICATION

For Anna

(The stage is divided into two living areas of adjacent condos. One has been fully remodeled. It's comfortable but every inch has been touched by someone with immaculate, modern sensibilities. The other apartment reflects an older, rural sensibility. Embroidery is popular here, as well as Jesus and doilies. The couch is covered with a plastic slipcover. Lights rise on the remodeled apartment. DONALD and RHONDA, two rural Texans in their sixties are the guests of MARCUS and CLARK, two fifty-ish gay men. MARCUS sits quietly with DONALD and RHONDA.)

(Pause)

DONALD: So…I've wanted to ask. Which— Which one of you is the wife?

(Beat)

And which is the husband?

(Pause)

MARCUS: We're both men, Donald. Like you.

DONALD: Right. Right, but who's the wife?

RHONDA: Don, it's 2015, that's not—that's not the right way to say that—

MARCUS: No. It's perfectly fine, Rhonda. I understand the—the origin of Donald's question. I know why you've asked it. In your experience, your frame of reference, in your life the couples you've known have followed a traditionally accepted model. One man and one woman, each fulfilling a traditional sex role. It's perfectly natural to wonder if my relationship with Clark fits into that familiar mold in some way. Well, there isn't a wife and a husband. He is my husband and I am his. Homosexuality does not imply femininity in any way, shape, or form.

(The door to the kitchen opens and CLARK *enters with dessert.)*

CLARK: Ta da! Who needs a little something sweet!?

RHONDA: Me!

CLARK: Girl, you are a little something sweet.

RHONDA: Did you hear that, Don?

DONALD: Uh, huh.

CLARK: Oh! Marcus has his professor face on. Did I walk into something?

RHONDA: No.

MARCUS: No, Donald just had a question about our lifestyle.

CLARK: Yay! What do you want to know? I'm ready to dish.

DONALD: It's okay.

MARCUS: He just wondered if, in our relationship, one of us took on the role of the wife and—

CLARK: Oh, that's me—

MARCUS: —Clark

CLARK: I thought that was obvious. Hello!
(Beat)
Not what Marcus said?

MARCUS: No.

RHONDA: It doesn't matter—

CLARK: I agree. Don't worry about him, he thinks my public behavior sets the image of homosexuals back fifty years—

MARCUS: —I do not—

CLARK: —But he fell in love with me for my private behavior and my public and private behavior happen to be exactly the same.

MARCUS: You are consistent.

CLARK: Anyhoo, dessert is served.
(He has given everyone a well dressed, individual serving of chocolate mousse.)

DONALD: Mmm, pudding. I like pudding.

MARCUS: Actually, it's a chocolate mousse.

DONALD: It looks like chocolate pudding.

RHONDA: It's different, dear.

CLARK: Tomato. Tomahto.

MARCUS: Actually…they are both creamy, dairy based…. They both use binding agents, corn starch, eggs, gelatin, what have you. The primary difference, and it's not insignificant, is that a mousse is delicate and airy because it's been gently whipped.

DONALD: Huh.

MARCUS: Or folded. And it's always served cold. This is a mousse.

(Beat. They all eat. It's good. Beat)

DONALD: It tastes like pudding.

CLARK: Yeah.

MARCUS: Nevertheless, it is a mousse.

(Pause)

CLARK: Let's get a little more comfortable? Let's move this party into the living room.

MARCUS: Excellent idea.

(CLARK *and* MARCUS *rise to cross into the living room, followed by* DONALD. RHONDA *stays seated.*)

RHONDA: But...

CLARK: Rhonda, you don't seem to be moving.

RHONDA: But the mousse—We're not done with dessert.

CLARK: Bring it with.

RHONDA: Oh, I, I couldn't— Your furniture... Your couch.

DONALD: She doesn't like messes.

RHONDA: I don't like messes.

CLARK: Then don't make a mess. We're all adults, I think we can handle our mousse.

MARCUS: It's fine.

CLARK: C'mon. Look—
(*He waves his mousse around, maybe does a little dance.*)
I'm dancing...with mousse...

RHONDA: Oh, my, that is so...cavalier—

CLARK: That's right. I'm being cavalier with mousse. I'm not worried about spilling and I don't think you will spill, either. I trust you, Rhonda.

RHONDA: Well...

CLARK: Come, join us.

RHONDA: Ohhh...
(*She rises.*)

CLARK: C'mon...

RHONDA: Your couch—it's white?

MARCUS: Actually, it's Ecru.

CLARK: Don't worry... come to the couch... come...

(RHONDA *starts, stops, grabs her napkin to put under her bowl and crosses slowly to the living area.*)

CLARK: Yes…Rhonda, you wild woman.

(RHONDA *perches uncomfortably on the couch.*)

CLARK: Excellent! Look at you, totally relaxed and natural.

(*Though that's not true,* RHONDA *smiles to herself, a little proud.*)

CLARK: I think everyone should always be comfortabl—whoa!

(CLARK *fakes dropping his mousse.* RHONDA *screams!*)

CLARK: I'm sorry. I'm sorry!

RHONDA: Don't do that! Oh, Lord in heaven! Oh!

CLARK: I'm so sorry! I couldn't resist.

RHONDA: That was not funny!

DONALD: That was pretty funny.

(*Beat*)

RHONDA: Thank you so much for having us over.

MARCUS: Of course, how long have you been next door, six months?

RHONDA: Almost six months.

MARCUS: It was past time to really get to know our neighbors.

RHONDA: Well… Other than Clark scaring me to death this has been lovely.

(*They all smile, confirm.*)

RHONDA: Real lovely. I just—just really nice of ya'll to have us at your condo, cook a nice supper, and this mousse. It's a mousse, Don. Don. Don is used to pudding.

CLARK: It has been nice.

RHONDA: Right Don? Supper was so lovely.

DONALD: It was good.

RHONDA: Thank you for having us. So, nice. What a great supper.

CLARK: Thank you!

RHONDA: Supper was just so good.

CLARK: Yes, it was.

(Beat)

RHONDA: Who knew we'd have so much to talk about?

DONALD: You talked about The Voice the whole time.

RHONDA: They like The Voice as much as I do.

CLARK: Love it. So glad X-Tina is back.

RHONDA: See, Don. They love X-Tina. Don loves her, too. What did you want to talk about, religion and politics? I don't think so, Don. My daddy always said, "Don't talk about religion or politics in mixed company" and you know, I do believe he was right.

MARCUS: I believe that, too.

(Beat)

RHONDA: What a fine night. A mighty fine night. The grilled salad—

MARCUS: Yes—

RHONDA: Who grills salad?

CLARK: But it totally works—

RHONDA: It was so good. You could taste the smoke. Right, Don? You could taste the smoke in the salad?

DONALD: I tasted smoke.

MARCUS: Thank you. Just a little recipe we picked up in Madrid.

RHONDA: Oh! Madrid! I'd love to visit Italy.

(Pause. CLARK and MARCUS are amused but decide not to pursue it.)

CLARK: Girl. I love your hair.

RHONDA: Oh? Oh!
(She laughs. Terribly flattered)

CLARK: I used to do hair so she knows of what she speaks.

DONALD: Huh.

CLARK: I know, right. The old queen used to do hair. Surprise! Not professionally but for this ol' gal that sang every Thursday night at the Hideaway—

MARCUS: Clark—

CLARK: Oh! She was fabulous! And what I did was very Sashay Shante. You remind me of her.

RHONDA: Really?! What was her name?

CLARK: Rachel.

RHONDA: Rachel—

CLARK: Rachel Tension.

RHONDA: Rachel Tension. That's pretty.

CLARK: Lord, what a diva.

RHONDA: Hear that Don? I have the hair of a diva. Sashay—what?

CLARK: Shante.

RHONDA: Sashay Shante, Don.

DONALD: Uh huh.

CLARK: Those were the days, weren't they, baby?

MARCUS: They were.

CLARK: Oh, Rachel… He was gorgeous.

RHONDA: Hmm?—

MARCUS: —Mmmm, this mousse.

(*They all make noises of pleasure as they eat.*)

CLARK: Oh, my.

RHONDA: It is good. So good!

DONALD: Tasty.

CLARK: Delicious—

RHONDA: Very—

MARCUS: Yes—

CLARK: Absolutely sinful.

RHONDA: Actually…I don't like to think of it as sinful.

CLARK: Honey, if you ate the whole bowl you'd wake up tomorrow morning with an extra thigh. It's sinful.

RHONDA: Well, no. It's not. I believe in the biblical definition of Sin… Sin is a willful rebellion against God. So, a good dessert doesn't qualify.
(*Beat*)
But we're not talking religion or politics. I mean we're a year away from an election. Nothing like talking politics to drive people apart.

CLARK: Well, I will support the new president. Whoever she may be.

(*Beat*)

MARCUS: Whomever.

CLARK: Where in East, Texas did you—

DONALD: Outside of Paris.

CLARK: Ooh, la la.

(RHONDA *laughs.*)

CLARK: Maisons-Laffitte,? Versailles, perhaps?

DONALD: No. County road 2143. We had twenty-five acres.

MARCUS: So, your daughter brought you to Dallas?

DONALD: Be closer to her—

RHONDA: And our new granddaughter!

DONALD: Our baby had a baby.

RHONDA: A little girl.

CLARK: Awwee—

RHONDA: And we wanted to watch her grow up. Be there to help. When it warms up, you'll see her out at the pool. Don's gonna teach her how to swim, aren't you Don?

DONALD: Mm-hmm—

RHONDA: I always say everybody's got to know how to swim.

DONALD: Right.
(Beat)
Can you swim, Marcus?

(Pause)

MARCUS: Yes. Donald. I can swim.

DONALD: Oh, sorry! I didn't mean—

RHONDA: He didn't mean you couldn't swim because you're—

MARCUS: —It's okay—

RHONDA: —Because you're a—

MARCUS: —I understand—

RHONDA: —Because you're a—blaa…

MARCUS: I understand. It's okay. You can say it. I am a blaafrican American.

(Beat)

CLARK: Oh, you're foolin'. He's foolin'. You're foolin'.

MARCUS: Am I?

CLARK: You are. You are.

RHONDA: Oh! Oh, good! Oh, Marcus. I thought we had a international incident!

MARCUS: No, no international incidents. We're all from here and it happened here.

RHONDA: Whew…well, yeah… It was an innocent question—

MARCUS: I know.

RHONDA: So, sorry.

MARCUS: It's okay. It's okay. I can swim.

(Pause)

CLARK: No you can't.

MARCUS: I can swim! Just because I don't swim often doesn't mean I cannot and even if I couldn't swim it doesn't enforce some antiquated cultural stereotype.

CLARK: Okay. Jeez. You're not good at swimming.

MARCUS: I chose not to master it.

DONALD: What if you fell off a boat?

MARCUS: I'd swim…slowly to safety.

(Beat)

CLARK: So…you're grandparents. We haven't—we haven't really talked enough about that.

RHONDA: Oh, yes. So happy. Just—just so happy.

MARCUS: So, you moved to Dallas for family. Why did you choose to move to Cedar Springs and Oaklawn?

CLARK: Yes. What possessed you?

DONALD: Cost.

RHONDA: We sold our house and our land and didn't want a mortgage so we looked at houses forever but everything is so expensive here.

DONALD: We had a four bedroom—

RHONDA: Four bedroom, three bath. We sold it to a nice, a real nice Hispanic couple, I mean, but they were real nice—and we looked for houses here and the only thing that money would buy outright was small, three bed, one bath, two bed one bath…

DONALD: And the neighborhoods. Rough.

CLARK: What neighborhoods?

DONALD: Almost got something in Oak Cliff.

CLARK: Oak Cliff is cute!

MARCUS: Oak Cliff is not rough anymore.

DONALD: Well, it was rough enough.

MARCUS: It's diverse.

DONALD: It was pretty rough.

RHONDA: So, we started looking at condos—

DONALD: No yard work. A little small but—

RHONDA: Nice pool—

DONALD: Neighborhood seemed nice enough.

CLARK: Have you noticed anything about the Cedar Springs neighborhood? Anything about the residents? The make up of all of the residents—

MARCUS: Clark—

CLARK: You moved into the heart of the gayborhood.

MARCUS: Plenty of heterosexuals live in this neighborhood.

CLARK: Not really.

MARCUS: That is just not true.

CLARK: I know two and I'm pretty sure they accidentally moved here.

RHONDA: We didn't notice when we were looking. I just thought, "I love rainbows!" I didn't know.

CLARK: You didn't notice all of the gay men?

RHONDA: We'd never met a gay man before so...

DONALD: Well—

RHONDA: What? Who?

DONALD: Buddy McWilliams—

RHONDA: What?

DONALD: He used to give me the creeps. Kind of look at you too long. Too much eye contact for a normal person.

CLARK: He was giving you the eye?

DONALD: He was giving me both eyes.

CLARK: Makes sense. I know as a gay man, I always make very strong eye contact with both eyes with all men. It's just how God made me.

DONALD: Right.

RHONDA: Buddy McWilliams that works at the Texaco?

DONALD: Owns the Texaco.

RHONDA: Oh, he does not own the Texaco. Cora Mae Stewart owns it now that her husband is passed. Buddy McWilliams just works there.

DONALD: Oh, I figured a man that age working at a filling station must own it.

RHONDA: Don, Buddy McWilliams ain't right in his head—

DONALD: What?

RHONDA: He was kicked in the head by a goat when he was a baby.

DONALD: He was what?

RHONDA: How did you not know that?!

DONALD: How am I supposed to know a baby goat kicked him in the head—

RHONDA: —No, he was a baby and a goat kicked him in the head—

DONALD: —Well, whatever—

RHONDA: The goat was a grown up—

DONALD: Okay—

RHONDA: People call him Bahhdy.

DONALD: Never understood that.

RHONDA: Cause he had his little head kicked in by his momma's mean old goat.

DONALD: Well, I'll be.

RHONDA: Yup. Sad. Sad.

(Pause)

CLARK: Lemme get this straight… So… Uh… The one gay man you thought you knew…was actually just kicked in the head…by a goat…

DONALD: Turns out…

MARCUS: …That's illuminating.

DONALD: I was confused about that whole thing, I guess.

RHONDA: You sure were.

CLARK: Well, now you've met two gay men who don't have brain damage. How's that feel?

RHONDA: Oh. Good. Real good.

DONALD: Yeah, good.

CLARK: We haven't given Don the eye once.

RHONDA: Oh, no!

CLARK: We've resisted the nearly overwhelming urge!

MARCUS: Clark—

CLARK: But if a goat gets in here and bashes our brains in I'm not making any promises!

RHONDA: Oh! Oh!

(The laugh crests then dies out.)

RHONDA: Oh, it's fun to laugh. But Don's always had to fight the ladies off with a stick.

(Beat. RHONDA *and* CLARK *laugh.)*

RHONDA: No, no. I'm teasing. He don't. But ol' Don's a good man, aren't you, Don?

DONALD: Yup.

(Beat)

MARCUS: How are you enjoying being grandparents?

RHONDA: Oh, I love it. I love it.

CLARK: I'd love to see her.

RHONDA: Oh. Oh, let me show you…

MARCUS: We love babies.

RHONDA: *(She gets out her phone.)* My daughter she—she texts me these photos—and let me see if I remember… Okay, here she is, climbing out from under the couch—

*(*CLARK *is taken aback.)*

CLARK: Whoa!

RHONDA: A doll, right?

CLARK: Yeah…yeah, she is a doll. A real doll. Look at this, Marcus.

MARCUS: Ah! She's a doll.

RHONDA: Now, we're—we're keeping her during the day when our daughter works so we get to go see that pumkin everyday.

CLARK: Marcus, do you remember when our baby was a baby?

MARCUS: I do.

CLARK: Ohhh, I miss those days. Now she's all, "I know everything!"

MARCUS: She damn near does. You're right Rhonda. The most special… cherished time of my life was when our daughter was say two—

CLARK: Three-ish.

MARCUS: When she was two. Oh, my god. There was absolutely nothing sweeter than reading her a book then rocking her to sleep.

CLARK: When she said "Dada" for the first time and we both claimed it.

MARCUS: She was looking at me.

CLARK: She was telling you about me.

(They're tickled, enjoying the memory.)

RHONDA: Are ya'll kidding? Ya'll have a baby?

CLARK: Well, she's almost twenty.

RHONDA: Oh… Really?

CLARK: Uh-huh.

RHONDA: How did you? How was she—

CLARK: Who got who pregnant?

MARCUS: We adopted her.

CLARK: Well, we raised her for years and then we adopted her and now she—

MARCUS: —Spends all of our money.

CLARK: Spends all of our money.

RHONDA: Well…huh…that's—that's nice.

CLARK: Yeah…of course, I long for the days when I spent all of our money.

MARCUS: Mm-hmm.

CLARK: So, look at the four of us. It seems we have more in common than it…seems.

MARCUS: Some notable differences.

DONALD: How did you get her?

CLARK: Hmm?

DONALD: How did you get her in the first place. You raised her before you adopted—

CLARK: Oh, little secret, she's Marcus's niece—

MARCUS: Clark! Damnit, you've got to stop doing that—

CLARK: She is!

MARCUS: Yes, and there's no reason for everyone in her life to know that when she doesn't—

CLARK: Donald and Rhonda are not in her life—

MARCUS: All the more damn reason. The— The damn neighbors know more about her origins that she does because you can't keep your damn mouth shut about it.

CLARK: Oooh… He's mad.

MARCUS: I'm not mad—

CLARK: —I know. You're not damn mad at all—

MARCUS: —I just don't know why you insist on telling everyone that part of her journey when we've decided—

CLARK: —You've decided—

MARCUS: —that it's best for her to believe she is my biological child and not my damn brother's. Sorry.

(Beat)

DONALD: Your brother a criminal or a drug addict?

(Beat)

MARCUS: What makes you think that, Donald?

CLARK: Honey, please—

MARCUS: No, Clark. What makes you assume my brother would be a drug addict?

DONALD: Oh…well, you don't want her raised by a drug crazed criminal…so you adopted her…to get her away from that… Just a guess. Am I wrong?

RHONDA: Whatever it is and you don't have to say another word about it, I think it's wonderful that you took that girl into your home and gave her a better life. And two daddies. That's fine with me.

CLARK: Oh?

RHONDA: I just wanted you to know that. Beats the heck outta no daddies.

CLARK: Oh, that's nice.

RHONDA: It just shows that you are kind, and generous people. Being a parent is the most selfless thing you can do.

CLARK: Amen.

MARCUS: Thank you, Rhonda.

RHONDA: Now let's talk about something else.

CLARK: Let's.

DONALD: I don't suppose you guys like sports?

CLARK: We love sports!

DONALD: Really?

CLARK: Absolutely. Gymnastics…dressage…
gymnastics.

DONALD: Oh.

MARCUS: He's kidding. We're huge Cowboys fans.

DONALD: Hey, hey. How bout them Cowboys?!

MARCUS: How bout 'em?

CLARK: How bout 'em?

(They all laugh. Sigh)

DONALD: In high school I used to play linebacker.

CLARK: Oh!? I used to be a tight end but one thing led
to another and—

(MARCUS hits CLARK.)

RHONDA: I'd like to say what I believe: This dinner is
a testament, a testament that very different people,
people from very different places and different ways of
thinking about the world can come together and have
a good time together in spite of their differences and
disagreements. I think the world could learn a lot from
us. From folks like us.

MARCUS: Well…

RHONDA: You may disagree and that's you're right,
Marcus. I may disagree with things about you, about
how you live your life, but that won't keep me from
seeing the good in you and lending you a Christian,
neighborly, friendly hand when you need one! That's
what I believe!

CLARK: Girl, you are wasted!

RHONDA: I am! I really am!

CLARK: Awesome. Oh! I'm on empty again. Lemme
refresh and we'll toast it up. Marcus? Anyone?

MARCUS: I'm good.

RHONDA: One's my limit.

CLARK: Suit yourselves. Don't come crying to me when I've finished the whole bottle by myself and take my pants off over my head.
(He pours but there's only a drop or two.)

MARCUS: I never do.

(CLARK hisses at MARCUS, like a cat.)

CLARK: New bottle, coming up. Rhonda?

RHONDA: Oh, why not.

CLARK: Excellent. I'll be back—Wanna help me choose a bottle?

RHONDA: Sure! And I'd love to see your kitchen! I love kitchens.

CLARK: We'll open some of the good stuff.

RHONDA: Ooh, good stuff. Have you heard of White Zinfandel?

(Beat)

CLARK: Yes.

RHONDA: Isn't it wonderful!?

CLARK: *(With a look to MARCUS)* Uh-huh.

(They're gone. Pause)

DONALD: So, asking about who the wife was—

MARCUS: Don't mention it—

DONALD: —No, I just want you to know that I didn't mean nothing by it—

MARCUS: I know.

DONALD: I was just curious how it worked.

MARCUS: Sure—

DONALD: I just meant if one of you was the wife, like if one of you does the cooking and the cleaning, and laundry, that sort of thing. So, you know, nothing offensive.

MARCUS: *(With a laugh)* Right—

DONALD: Not who does what to who—

MARCUS: Okay—

DONALD: And who does the doing, if you know what I mean?

MARCUS: Believe me, I understand.

DONALD: And your brother; on that one—I just been watching too much Law and Order.

MARCUS: Look, I've been discriminated against in some form or fashion for my entire life so I guess I'm conditioned to look for it, or expect it. It makes me angry and I—It's okay , Don.

DONALD: Good. Cause, I am a good guy.

MARCUS: I can tell.

DONALD: Good. And I don't care who is what race. I don't.

MARCUS: Good. Me either.

DONALD: Or who votes for who.

MARCUS: Free country.

DONALD: Right. Free country. Obama's not the worst thing that's ever happened. There, I said it… It could be worse.

MARCUS: It certainly could be.
(Beat)
It could be a lot worse.

DONALD: A lot… So… you like sports?

MARCUS: I do.

DONALD: What sport did you play?

MARCUS: I didn't play any sport.

DONALD: What? Really?

MARCUS: Really.

DONALD: Really? Not even basketball?

MARCUS: No, Donald, not even basketb—See, now…

DONALD: I bet you would have been good at basketball.

MARCUS: …Oh…god… See—okay, why is it about me that makes you think I'd be good at basketball?

(Beat)

DONALD: You're…tall.

(Pause. MARCUS has crossed to a small snack tray.)

MARCUS: Cracker.

DONALD: What?

MARCUS: Would you like a cracker?

(RHONDA and CLARK reenter.)

CLARK: Let the party recommence!

RHONDA: Party! Woo. Oh, I haven't had two glasses of wine in years. Oh, are my cheeks flushed?

DONALD: Yes.

RHONDA: Oh, Don. Don is a teetotaler.

CLARK: And I'm a Capricorn!

RHONDA: …That's great!

CLARK: Okay. Raise your glass, whatever is in it. I think this has been an educational and, all in all, a pleasant evening. A wise man once said, "There isn't anyone you couldn't learn to love once you've heard their story."

RHONDA: That's nice. Who said that?

CLARK: Mr Rogers.

(CLARK *and* MARCUS's *daughter,* SOPHIA *enters carrying a duffle bag full of dirty clothes. While she talks, she empties the bag onto the dining room table, sorts it somewhat, and pours herself a big glass of wine. She's very charming, but beside herself.*)

SOPHIA: So, Chase, like anyone has ever had a good relationship with a guy named Chase— We're at the movies, we've been "dating" for, what, a month, we've probably slept together fifty times—

MARCUS: —Honey—

SOPHIA: —at least, and this dude shows me his new— and mind you this is just as the movie is starting—he rolls up his sleeve , "Huh, huh, look", and shows me that he got an Iron Man tattoo. Iron Man. Fucking Iron Man. It hits me that I am dating a dude named after a bank who got an Iron Man tattoo.

MARCUS: Sophe—

(SOPHIA *notices* RHONDA *and* DONALD.)

SOPHIA: So— Do you guys see the people sitting there?

MARCUS: Yes. They're our guests.

(MARCUS *takes* SOPHIA's *wine away from her.*)

SOPHIA: Oh! Good! I was worried you were ghosts! I see white people!

RHONDA: Oh! We're alive!

SOPHIA: Great! So, I asked him, "Why would you do that to you're body?" He said, "Iron Man is cool." I'm like, "Grow a fucking goatee then. Don't permanently scar your body with a cartoon character. I beg of you, I say, you are too intelligent, I know your spirit is too deep to spend the rest of your life with everyone who sees your left arm thinking you must have gotten a tattoo when you were five years old—

RHONDA: It doesn't seem very mature.

CLARK: —Sophe, we're—

SOPHIA: He's like, Uhhh" and I'm like, "All you have to say is Uhh? How is our generation going to EVER be taken seriously if we are obsessed with some adolescent gun porn fantasy? What is it about guys and guns?! This dude's whole fucking body is a gun and he's your hero? Hero. Bullfuckingshit. You think Iron Man is a hero? Try Malala Yousafzai. What she stands in the face of would make Iron Man's dick crawl back inside his body and try to make an escape out of his butt." You know what I mean?

RHONDA: Well—

SOPHIA: Then he got up, said, "I'm breaking up with you," and left. And then the whole theater applauded for some reason.

MARCUS: Honey, these are our new neighbors Donald and Rhonda.

SOPHIA: Hi.

RHONDA: Hi.

SOPHIA: Are you rich?

RHONDA: Um-No—

SOPHIA: Then why do you vote against your own self interests?

(Beat)

CLARK: Donald, Rhonda, this is our daughter, Sophia—

MARCUS: She's an idiot.

CLARK: Since she found out she has a high-ish I Q she's gotten dumber and dumber.

RHONDA: Well, it's nice to meet you, Sophia. That is a pretty name. We had a weenie dog named Sophia.

SOPHIA: What a beautiful compliment.

CLARK: We're having them over to officially welcome them to the neighborhood.

SOPHIA: Sweet. How do you like it so far?

RHONDA: It's just great.

SOPHIA: It is, right? You're not afraid of being straight bashed?

MARCUS: Sophe—

CLARK: She's joking. And don't mind her. She's a psychology major. She likes to push people towards extreme emotions and then study how they react. It's annoying. Ignore it.

SOPHIA: I'm a student of human behavior. Also, I'm a double major. Psychology and political science. How many guns do you guys own?

MARCUS: —Don't answer that—

DONALD: Six—

SOPHIA: Ha! Six!

CLARK: Don't start, Sophe.

SOPHIA: I was just making sure they had an arsenal to defend themselves in case they're straight bashed.

CLARK: *(To* RHONDA *and* DONALD*)* There's no such thing.

SOPHIA: It could happen.

CLARK: Sophia, before you arrived we were having a polite, civilized conversation.

SOPHIA: Okay—

CLARK: And then you come in and it's like you're firing sarcastic tweets at them.

SOPHIA: They're—

CLARK: No, you're—

SOPHIA: —I can't have an open political conversation with our guests?

CLARK: No.

MARCUS: No.

SOPHIA: We talk about politics all the time.

MARCUS: Not in front of company, we don't.

SOPHIA: Oh, so repress it?

MARCUS: Absolutely.

SOPHIA: I get it. Mixed company.

MARCUS: Right. This isn't Facebook.

SOPHIA: I don't do Facebook—

MARCUS: Whatever—

SOPHIA: Facebook is for old people—

MARCUS: Nap Chap ~ or whatever.

SOPHIA: ~ Snap Chat. Nap Chap ~

MARCUS: You can't just say everything you think in front of people.

SOPHIA: Okay, Jesus Christ.
(She takes CLARK's mousse and throws herself onto the couch. She eats.)

CLARK: Sorry, about that, ya'll.

RHONDA: It's okay. We raised a daughter. She slammed the doors off the hinges.

DONALD: Lots of door slamming.

CLARK: I do not miss the slamming of the doors.

SOPHIA: I grew out of that.

CLARK: Mostly—

SOPHIA: Mostly.

MARCUS: What I find interesting—and Sophia, you missed most of this, but you could learn something. What I find interesting is that on the surface, just based on archetypal assumptions, we seem opposites. But with discourse over a shared meal we find we have much in common.

SOPHIA: You guys are Cowboys fans.

DONALD: Yep.

CLARK: Rhonda and I both love rainbows.

RHONDA: Sure do!

MARCUS: We both parented a door slamming daughter.

SOPHIA: Slamming doors is merely a physical manifestation of psychic pain.

MARCUS: I always thought it was a physical manifestation of being a brat.

SOPHIA: Being a brat is a physical manifestation of psychic pain.

MARCUS: You are a turd.

SOPHIA: I love you daddy.
(She slides in and hugs him.)

MARCUS: Oh. I love you too, baby.

SOPHIA: Oh, daddy.

RHONDA: That's nice. Oh, that's so nice. That-you hugging like that is just as sweet as can be. I can't remember the last time Dolores hugged one of us voluntarily. Snuggled in like that. Well, Don is not real huggable.

DONALD: Nope.

RHONDA: But I'd like a hug every now and then. Guess you don't get that back if it goes away.

MARCUS: Well, Sophia has always been attached to us.

RHONDA: That's nice.

MARCUS: Studies show most only children brought up in a good environment stay very close to their parents as adults.

RHONDA: Well, Dolores isn't an onl—

DONALD: Nm—Con-Nm, Mm.

RHONDA: Mm.

(Beat)

SOPHIA: That. Was. Weird.

(RHONDA starts crying.)

SOPHIA: Je suis intrigué!

RHONDA: It's not— It's okay. I— We have a son, too. Dolores isn't an only child.

MARCUS: Ah. Okay.

DONALD: Rhonda. Damnit. This is why I didn't want you to drink wine—

RHONDA: He was our surprise baby—

DONALD: It's—that's private information—

SOPHIA: It's private information that you have a son?

RHONDA: No.

DONALD: I just don't want to talk about it—

RHONDA: Twelve years younger than his sister—

DONALD: Rhonda—

RHONDA: Surprise! You're parents again!

DONALD: Awe, hell.

RHONDA: We think he's troubled.

DONALD: Damnit, Rhonda—

MARCUS: Oh, I'm sorry.

DONALD: Nothing to be sorry about. He's just… troubled. And that's okay—

RHONDA: And that's okay. The Lord has a plan. He's really a sweet boy. Ronnie. His name is Ronnie.

CLARK: He lives with you?

RHONDA: Yes. I home school him. We're almost finished, he's fixin' to be eighteen, but I think he's not really ready to venture out of the nest yet. The world is such a scary place.

CLARK: I'm sure he is.

(SOPHIA *rises and crosses to the door.*)

CLARK: Where are you going?

SOPHIA: Out.
(*She exits.*)

RHONDA: She's a very pretty girl.

MARCUS: Thank you. She is that. Sorry about her grilling you about, you know, political stuff. Asking about your guns—

CLARK: She's an "activist". She "Cares about things." It's annoying.

DONALD: It's okay. We're responsible gun owners.

CLARK: I'm sure you are.

DONALD: Keep 'em put up, treat 'em with respect and they won't hurt anyone.

(*Blackout on their apartment. Lights up on* RHONDA *and* DONALD'S *apartment.* RONNIE, *their son is sitting on the couch playing with or looking at the gun. Looks at it thoughtfully. There's a knock on the door. It shocks him. He waits and there is another knock. He rises, puts the gun in the front of his pants, covers it with his shirt, and crosses to the door. He opens it and* SOPHIA *enters.*)

SOPHIA: Ronnie!

(She gives him a big hug and continues into the room.)

RONNIE: Uhh…

(Pause)

SOPHIA: Oh no, are you retarded?

RONNIE: Umm…

(Beat)

No.

SOPHIA: Ah! Good. Sorry. Intellectually disabled. Are you intellectually disabled?

RONNIE: I'm not.

SOPHIA: Good. Look at this place. Interior design by Cracker Barrel. Oh, and a couch condom. Cool!

RONNIE: Who are you?

SOPHIA: I'm Sophia— So, I could just sit down and pee and the couch would be okay?
(She sits.)

RONNIE: I believe so.

(Beat)

SOPHIA: Shy bladder.

RONNIE: Why are you here? How do you know my name?

SOPHIA: I was sent by God, Ronnie.

RONNIE: What?

SOPHIA: God sent me to save you. Said you were troubled.

RONNIE: Well…fuck him.

SOPHIA: Her. Fuck her. God is a lady, Ronnie. Instead of a big beard, she has big hair. It's a perm… No, I'm— I'm your neighbor, Ronnie. I'm— Your parents are at my house right now having dinner with my two dads.

RONNIE: Oh…umm… Right. Okay.

SOPHIA: Hi.

RONNIE: Hi.

SOPHIA: Can I ask you a question? Answer as if you were a white person.

RONNIE: I'll try.

SOPHIA: Do you believe we're evolving socially? Like the polls that suggest each generation is getting more and more tolerant of people that are different? Less racist, less homophobic, less whatever, on average. I mean Dallas has a lesbian Latina for a Sheriff. We have a black president. Our parents are blinded by their own shit but we have a chance to see each other as just two humans rather than members of different tribes and our kids should make us look like intolerant pricks. Right? That's the trend right?

RONNIE: Umm—I don't know. Maybe.

SOPHIA: Or do you believe it's getting worse.

RONNIE: I don't know.

SOPHIA: Me either. Maybe the tribes are just shifting.

RONNIE: Maybe.

SOPHIA: Yeah, yeah… I really shook you up. Sorry.

RONNIE: I'm fine.

SOPHIA: You're shaky.

RONNIE: I'm okay.

SOPHIA: Okay. Okay. Your parents are nice people. They loved me.

RONNIE: Um…yeah? Really?

SOPHIA: Hey, you got anything to drink in here?

RONNIE: We have some Sunny D, some purple stuff…

(SOPHIA *gives* RONNIE *a look.*)

RONNIE: Oh…I…umm, I have some vodka hidden in my room.

SOPHIA: Vodka? Nothing stronger?

RONNIE: No. I'll go get it.

(RONNIE *exits.* SOPHIA *inspects the room, looking at all of the pictures. He reenters with a small bottle of vodka.*)

RONNIE: I'll get you a glass.

SOPHIA: Glasses are for pussies.
(*She takes a chug.*)

RONNIE: Oh, yeah…I usually use a glass—

SOPHIA: Have a drink.

(RONNIE *takes a drink.*)

SOPHIA: Let's make it a big boy drink.

(RONNIE *takes a bigger drink.* SOPHIA *takes it back and takes another drink.*)

SOPHIA: Can I ask you a question? Are you really troubled?

RONNIE: No. Can I ask you a question?

SOPHIA: Shoot.

RONNIE: Did you really try to pee on my couch?

SOPHIA: Yes.

RONNIE: Are you troubled?

She laughs.

SOPHIA: Your parents really are nice.

RONNIE: Yeah.

SOPHIA: They're part of a backwards faction of the last generation that is holding this country back in every imaginable way but, yes. Very lovely people. They are exactly as they seem.

RONNIE: They are.

SOPHIA: Are you?

RONNIE: I am not.

SOPHIA: That's it. "I am not." Is this a record player?

RONNIE: It is.

SOPHIA: Love it. Anything good?

She locates and starts going through the records.

RONNIE: Like, what do you think is good?

SOPHIA: This is some sexy shit. I mean, I don't really like any of it but it's old, and it makes me seem more worldly if I'm into old records. Are you buying it?

RONNIE: Well…not now.

SOPHIA: Some of this is— Do your parents have deceptively groovy taste in music?

RONNIE: Oh. No. They buy all the records they can find at garage sales. My mom thinks she's going to make a fortune on Antiques Road Show.

SOPHIA: That explains this…
(She puts on a song and dances towards him.)

RONNIE: Yeah, that's pretty groovy.

SOPHIA: Dance with me, Ronnie.

RONNIE: I'm no good at dancing.

SOPHIA: Dance man, dance. Let it all go. Just be free.

(SOPHIA dances. RONNIE slowly joins in. He's comically awkward. She laughs. He picks up a picture frame and throws it on the ground.)

RONNIE: I told you I couldn't dance! I told you!

SOPHIA: I'm sorry! I'm sorry! Hey—

RONNIE: You made me dance just to laugh at me—

SOPHIA: No, no, Ronnie, no—I didn't. I just wanted to dance with you, I swear…. I just laughed because you were so bad—

RONNIE: Oh, fuck—

SOPHIA: No, now! What the does it matter if you can't dance!? I don't care. I probably enjoyed the laugh more than I would have enjoyed dancing. Seriously. Come here and sit down. More vodka.

(RONNIE *sits with* SOPHIA *and drinks.*)

SOPHIA: Take some more.

(RONNIE *drinks more.*)

SOPHIA: One more.

(RONNIE *drinks again.*)

SOPHIA: Good. Alcohol helps everything. So, you really lashed out there. Lie down. Just… Okay, just lie down. Lie down here, good. Just relax. Let all of that wash off of you. What were you feeling?

RONNIE: Umm… Why?

SOPHIA: I'm curious.
(*She takes out a note pad and a pen.*)
You had a moment where you slammed the picture down, when I was laughing. Can you describe how you were feeling?

RONNIE: No. Mad.

SOPHIA: Mad. Ok. And you couldn't just tell me to fuck off, you had to break something. Why?

RONNIE: Umm…I don't know.

SOPHIA: Yes you do.

RONNIE: Because—Because I was—you hurt my feelings, and I wanted…

SOPHIA: Did you want to hurt me?

(*Pause*)

RONNIE: No. No.

SOPHIA: How troubled are you? What meds are you on, Ronnie—

RONNIE: I'm not on any—are you taking notes?!

SOPHIA: It's for class!

RONNIE: Did my—Did my parents tell you I was troubled?

SOPHIA: Your Mom got super drunk on one glass of wine and told us all about it.

RONNIE: Man, fuck them! FUCK! They just go—I'm here and they just go somewhere and tell some people—just some strangers—FUCK! FUCK! FUUUUCCCKKK!

(*Beat*)

SOPHIA: Are you feeling angry now, Ronnie?

RONNIE: What's your deal?!

SOPHIA: I'm a student of human behavior. Look, I feel for you, man. If those were my parents, nice but all tight-assed and judgey, repressed, and bigoted... I mean, look at me, I'm a nightmare and I had an awesome childhood. If I'd had a bad one who knows how unbearable I'd be. Well, I mean...actually, my dad is a total derelict, drug addict and I was raised by my uncle and his husband. Don't tell anyone I know that. Clark told me but he wasn't suppose to.
(*Beat*)
What's it like to be home schooled?

RONNIE: Sucks!

SOPHIA: Have you always been home schooled?

RONNIE: No. I went to public school until the ninth grade.

SOPHIA: Why the change?

RONNIE: None of your business.

SOPHIA: Okay. Like, what do you learn?

RONNIE: Stuff.

SOPHIA: Stuff.

RONNIE: School stuff.

SOPHIA: No offense but every home schooled kid I ever met seemed like a fucking freak of nature.

RONNIE: Why would I take offense to that?

SOPHIA: But you're different. You're kind of cool seeming.

RONNIE: Really?

SOPHIA: Yeah, or like you could be cool… Not exactly what I was expecting from what your parents said.

RONNIE: They've got no idea.

SOPHIA: You're also kinda on the hot side.

RONNIE: No way.

SOPHIA: Way. Not half bad. Overall.

RONNIE: You're not half bad either.

SOPHIA: Oh!! And smooth! Home Schooler's got game. I gotta watch you.

RONNIE: I—gotta watch you, too.

SOPHIA: Less smooth. How old are you?

RONNIE: Eighteen.

SOPHIA: Oh, god, eighteen. You baby. I remember when I was eighteen.

RONNIE: How old are you?

SOPHIA: Almost twenty. So, what's you're malfunction?

(SOPHIA *sits close enough to* RONNIE *that he notices.*)

RONNIE: What—

SOPHIA: What's your problem? Why are you home schooled? Why do your parents tell everyone they meet that you're troubled?

RONNIE: Shit. I'm—I don't know.

SOPHIA: Do you want to get out of this house?

RONNIE: Yes.

SOPHIA: Why?

RONNIE: Because it's—

(RONNIE *gestures for* SOPHIA *to look around.*)

SOPHIA: I gotcha.

RONNIE: Hey, can I ask you a question? Do you hate your parents?

(*Beat*)

SOPHIA: No way. I love them. I mean, I guess it's fucked up that they're my only friends… But parents are just part of the problem, right? Do you hate yourself?

RONNIE: Huh?

SOPHIA: You heard me.

RONNIE: No.

SOPHIA: Ha. Come on.

RONNIE: I don't know—what about you? Huh? What's your problem?

SOPHIA: C'mon, dude. I don't have any problems. Look at me.

RONNIE: Okay.

SOPHIA: Look. I know I'm not the smartest person
in the world but—I'm pretty sure I'm the smartest
person I know. And really pretty. I know I'm super
intimidating. Obviously, I'm killin' it… But, I mean…
like everybody wonders… "Am I more than where I
came from?"Am I just a collection of cells motivated
by chemicals programmed when a loser's sperm found
an egg? I mean, I used to fantasize about my dad and
mom showing up. Clean. Changed. Wanting me. Like
they 'd only stayed away because they were ashamed
of their past, and they'd finally gotten the courage to
let me see them. And I'd absolve them. And they'd be
so grateful that I'm so together…I'm already addicted
to making myself feel good… Every time I have a drink
or jump into bed with some rando dude, I feel doomed,
repeating their history. So, who am I seeing when I
look in the mirror and feel such loathing?

RONNIE: Yeah.

SOPHIA: That makes sense to you?

RONNIE: Yeah.

SOPHIA: Who am I? Who am I becoming? Right?

RONNIE: Right.

SOPHIA: What am I worth? Does anyone love me?

RONNIE: Right.

SOPHIA: Like—really love me? Right?

RONNIE: Right.

(Beat)

SOPHIA: You just want to be loved.

RONNIE: Yeah… Yes. Exactly.

*(Pause. SOPHIA puts another record on. It's kind of sexy.
She moves with it.)*

SOPHIA: Can I ask you a question?

RONNIE: ...Yeah...

SOPHIA: At your home school, did you have Sex Ed?

RONNIE: Oooh, boy...

SOPHIA: Sexual Education? Does your mommy teach you Sex Ed?

RONNIE: No.

SOPHIA: I'm a super qualified instructor.

RONNIE: Oooh, boy.

SOPHIA: I'm going to kiss you, Ronnie.

RONNIE: That's cool—

(RONNIE *and* SOPHIA *kiss. She pushes him down on the couch and straddles him. As soon as she lands on him she's surprised. She feels the gun in the front of his pants but she doesn't know it—)*

SOPHIA: Oh, Ronnie. You are...wow...that has got to be the...oh my, god...

RONNIE: Be careful...

SOPHIA: Mmm, sorry. Afraid you're going to shoot early?

RONNIE: Sort of—

(SOPHIA *kisses* RONNIE.)

SOPHIA: I have much to teach you.

RONNIE: Umm...hold—hold on.

SOPHIA: What?

RONNIE: We don't have to.

SOPHIA: I want to.

RONNIE: No—No. I want to but... We can talk a little more if you want.

SOPHIA: I was just talking about myself.

RONNIE: I liked it. I don't...I don't really...talk...to people. About anything...but definitely not about, like, real stuff.

SOPHIA: Oh.

RONNIE: Can we just...hang out some more or...? Is that cool?

SOPHIA: Yes, Ronnie. That's super cool.

(The door opens and DONALD *and* RHONDA *enter. She screams.)*

DONALD: What the hell!?

SOPHIA: Ah!

RONNIE: Mom, dad!

RHONDA: You get—you get away from my boy!

*(*SOPHIA *dismounts and quickly crosses away as* RHONDA *rushes to* RONNIE.*)*

RONNIE: Mom—

RHONDA: Oh, my baby, are you okay?!

SOPHIA: We were just dry humping!

RHONDA: Oh, my baby—

*(*CLARK *and* MARCUS *enter.* CLARK *brought his wine.)*

CLARK: We heard a scream!

MARCUS: Oh, no...

DONALD: Your daughter was attacking my son!

SOPHIA: His tongue was attacking my tonsils—

DONALD: You shut up!

CLARK: Whoa! Now, let's calm down.

RHONDA: No! I will not calm down! I held my tongue, but your, your daughter is a dirty, mean, stupid slut!

SOPHIA: I am not stupid!

DONALD: I knew you people were like this.

MARCUS: What do you mean you people?

CLARK: Marcus—

MARCUS: No, Donald made several suggestive comments tonight and I let him off the hook—

DONALD: Your daughter is trash. Is that suggestive enough for ya?

MARCUS: You better watch your mouth—

DONALD: Or what—

CLARK: —Marcus!

MARCUS: If I was a violent man I'd beat your old ass—

CLARK: Marc—

(DONALD *and* MARCUS *step towards each other,* CLARK *and* RHONDA *rush to get between them—*)

MARCUS: My daughter's trash?! You pretend your son doesn't even exist—

DONALD: He's troubled! And that's okay!

MARCUS: No it's not, you dumbass!

(MARCUS *and* DONALD *grab each other and wrestle.*)

RHONDA: Oh, god, they're wrasslin!

SOPHIA: Daddy, Stop!

(CLARK *and* RONNIE *move to break things up. During the scuffle the gun falls out of* RONNIE's *pants. The action stops. There's a general gasp.*)

SOPHIA: Your dick was a gun?

RONNIE: Yeah.

RHONDA: Oh, my baby—

SOPHIA: You could have shot my pussy off—

RONNIE: I know. I'm sorry.

DONALD: Boy—

RHONDA: —Oh, my baby… Please…not again—
(He grabs the gun and separates himself from the group.)
I wasn't doing anything—

RHONDA: *(To* DONALD*)* Please tell me it's not loaded.

DONALD: …We live in a city now. There are gangs—

RHONDA: We talked about this happening again.

MARCUS: Your troubled son carries a gun around?

RHONDA: We hide it and he keeps finding it.

RONNIE: Stop! Stop telling people I'm troubled! Do you want me to be insane!?

RHONDA: —No—

RONNIE: Do you want me to be insane?

RHONDA: Baby—

RONNIE: I'm not!

RHONDA: We're know you're not insane! Just please put the gun down before you do something crazy!

RONNIE: Like this? Is that what you think?
(He puts it under his chin.)
Is this how you picture me?

RHONDA: Baby, no!

RONNIE: Maybe I should—

RHONDA: No—

RONNIE: I can't live like this anymore—

RHONDA: What-what haven't we done for you?

RONNIE: This is so embarrassing—

RHONDA: We love you so much—

RONNIE: THAT DOESN'T MATTER!

SOPHIA: He's depressed—

DONALD: We know you're troubled—

RHONDA: —And that's okay—

DONALD: —That's okay. But you just need to suck it up, get your act together and put the gun down. Now, boy!

RONNIE: Daddy, please don't.

CLARK: This is horrible.
(He's just as on edge as everyone else but he takes a drink.)

RHONDA: You have parents who love you. You have a home. And food!

DONALD: Taco ring.

RHONDA: You want a taco ring, baby?

RONNIE: I don't want a taco ring!

RHONDA: I have all the ingredients. I could just whip it up—

RONNIE: Why are you so—God!

RHONDA: So many people in this world—the little, little kids in China or think about the terrible lives of the children in Africa—
(To MARCUS)
…No offense, Marcus.
(Back to RONNIE)
Or Mexico. God! Mexico! They want nothing more than what you have and you're going to throw it away.

RONNIE: I don't want anything I have.

DONALD: I didn't think you were this weak, Ronnie.

RONNIE: Dad—

DONALD: I didn't. Everybody gets sad. Clark, are you sad?

CLARK: Absolutely.
(He drinks.)

DONALD: Nobody is happy with anything. Ever. That's just part of life. It ain't getting any easier, I can tell you that. You just gotta learn to suck it up. If you can't do that then maybe you're just not as tough as I thought you were—

SOPHIA: Oh, Jesus fucking-! Suck it up?

DONALD: You don't know anything about this—

SOPHIA: I know it's not little league baseball. Ronnie, rub some dirt on your depression and get back out there—

DONALD: We're try—

SOPHIA: Maybe all Ronnie needs is to get out of this house? Huh? Maybe the one thing he needed, the thing that would change all of this would be to have some really nasty sex with a beautiful black coed—

RHONDA: You need to—

RONNIE: No, Mom!
(Beat)
Let her talk.
(Beat)

SOPHIA: Maybe my magical vagina could save Ronnie's life. Or maybe he just needs to hang out with someone who knows what it feels like to feel fucked up. Ronnie is a—I think just a run of the mill "my life sucks, I hate everything, why don't girls like me" type of depressive. Right, Ronnie?

RONNIE: I don't know—

SOPHIA: A little time and understanding and therapy could—

DONALD: He doesn't need to see some shrink.

SOPHIA: He's just had a gun under his chin—

RONNIE: I'm not crazy—

SOPHIA: Yeah, you are! Everybody is. And that's okay! It really is. I'm crazy, too. Look. Look—
(*She reaches in her purse and pulls out a bottle of pills.*)
I have to take these little guys to fix what's wrong with me. It was a long, hard search to find these particular pills— The side effects—

CLARK: She was a slave to the toilet—

SOPHIA: Okay—

CLARK: —Diarrhea—

SOPHIA: Right. Anyway... So, Ronnie, I really, man, I do know how you feel. And I think you are an awesome guy. You're cute and funny. You've got a totally excellent life ahead of you. I promise. So, are you really going to shoot yourself?

RONNIE: No.

SOPHIA: Fuckinay. What are you doing tomorrow night?

RONNIE: What?

SOPHIA: Wanna go to a movie sometime?

RONNIE: Yeah, I'd really like that.

(RONNIE *puts the gun on the ground in front of him and squats down, covering his face.* SOPHIA *crouches with him.*)

RHONDA: Oh, thank you, Jesus.

SOPHIA: You can call me, Sophia.

MARCUS: That was amazing.

Rhonda goes to Ronnie and hugs him.

RHONDA: Oh, my, baby.
(*To the room*)
I would like to hereby declare that I am now a gun control advocate!

DONALD: Let's not get carried away.

RHONDA: I told you! I told him! I told him we should get rid of the guns—

DONALD: I will not be blamed for this. My daddy gave me that pistol. I've had it since 1961—

RHONDA: And your son just pointed it in his own face in front of us and our gay neighbors!

DONALD: I know, but...I don't know. That's not my fault. It's just not. I don't want anything bad to happen... But... How else am I going to protect my fam—
(He breaks down. He's trying be a man but he just can't. He fights it. It's an awkward battle.)

CLARK: Is he having a heart attack?

RHONDA: I think he's crying. Oh, Don—

(RHONDA goes to DONALD and grabs him. She pulls him to RONNIE. RONNIE stands to meet them.)

RONNIE: I'm sorry, Daddy—

(DONALD pulls RONNIE into a hug, then they hold each other as a family.)

SOPHIA: Think we should probably...

MARCUS: Yes, let's—

CLARK: Oh—oh. Hey... Um, what's a taco ring?

RHONDA: Oh, it's taco filling; taco seasoned meat and bacon and cheese wrapped in a Pillsbury crescent roll dough and baked.

DONALD: It's real good.

RHONDA: Want me to write the recipe down?

CLARK: No, thanks.

MARCUS: Here, lemme just...
(He has picked up the gun and is struggling to unload it.)
God damn it.

DONALD: Whoa, whoa…

MARCUS: What?

DONALD: Let's just— Why don't you just put the gun down? You—

MARCUS: Oh, my god! I was trying to get it unloaded so you people don't—

DONALD: Look, just—just calm down—

MARCUS: —calm down?—

DONALD: —and put the gun down.

MARCUS: Are you seri-? Black man with a gun makes you more nervous than insane kid with a gun—

DONALD: That's not what I—

MARCUS: Yes, it is! God, I'm sick of your shit—

CLARK: Marcus, don't worry about it.

MARCUS: It's easy for you to not worry about it, Clark. But I'm fucking worried about this plague on our society.

DONALD: You sayin' I'm a plague on society?

MARCUS: Yes! Your behavior is a symptom of a vile malignancy; a debilitating, deeply pervasive sickness bringing our culture to its knees.

RHONDA: Well, that's not nice.

MARCUS: Your undiagnosed bipolar son just waived this gun around and when I pick it up, ME, an intelligent, mentally stable college professor with three degrees; a man who has never even pushed another person, when I pick it up to make the situation we're leaving behind a little safer, suddenly it's, "Hey, put that down. Why don't you just calm down and listen to reason." I AM THE REASONABLE ONE, MOTHERFUCKER!

SOPHIA: Daddy!

MARCUS: Unreasonable is leaving a loaded gun in a house with an untreated depressive!

CLARK: Oh, shit, the gloves are off—

MARCUS: And that picture of your grand baby scared the shit out of me.

CLARK: Marcus, put the gloves back on!

MARCUS: It's like something from a Japanese horror movie. What kind of baby crawls out from under a couch!? And Rhonda, can the religious shit. I'm not going to even get into the fact that your magic man in the sky is the most ludicrous invention in the history of mankind!

(He's using the gun to gesture as he gets angrier.)

CLARK: Marcus, the gun—

MARCUS: You invoke Jesus into everything, but I think his main message was to not judge other people, but you ignore that part don't you!? You ignore all the parts you don't like. Laying with a man is an abomination but mmm this bacon I put on EVERYTHING is delicious. You've judged us all night long—

RHONDA: —We have not!—

MARCUS: —your entire—people like you—your entire existence is about judging other people! Both of you! No matter what you say during polite conversation I know you hate us because we're gay, you hate me because I'm black, you hate our daughter because she's a slut—

SOPHIA: Daddy!

MARCUS: The thing that scares you most about this gun is that a brother is holding it! If either of you white pieces of shit, you fucking white pieces of shit

had a shred of mature self awareness you'd realize
the people in your lives most deserving of hatred
are yourselves and your shrivelled, bigoted dried up
cunts—

RHONDA: We are not bigots, you nigger!

(*Gasp. Beat.* MARCUS *points the gun at* RHONDA *for a moment which frightens everyone, including* MARCUS. *He leaves the apartment with the gun.* CLARK *follows him.*)

CLARK: Marcus. Honey—

(RHONDA *exits towards her kitchen.* DONALD *follows, leaving* SOPHIA *and* RONNIE *alone.*)

DONALD: Rhonda…

RONNIE: That was fucked up.

SOPHIA: That was awesome.

RONNIE: What was awesome about that?

SOPHIA: Don't you think the honesty was refreshing?

RONNIE: No.

SOPHIA: How are you feeling?

RONNIE: Umm, I don't know.

SOPHIA: Really. Suicidal?

RONNIE: …No. I was, I wasn't going to shoot myself.

SOPHIA: Really? Why did you have the gun?

RONNIE: I don't know. I was—I just like messing with it.

SOPHIA: You were playing with a loaded gun?

RONNIE: …Guns are awesome.

SOPHIA: So, you're not suicidal, you're just stupid?

RONNIE: Basically.

SOPHIA: Promise?

RONNIE: Yeah. Totally.

SOPHIA: And then with your parents?

RONNIE: I hate that they think that I would shoot myself.

SOPHIA: So you threatened to shoot yourself.

RONNIE: Basically.

(Beat)

SOPHIA: Think your Mom is okay?

RONNIE: No. Think your dad is okay?

SOPHIA: No. Jesus… Do you wanna sneak into your room and…cuddle?

RONNIE: Cuddle?

SOPHIA: It's like hugging while laying down. It'll make you feel better. We're studying it's therapeutic effects in Human Intimacy and Development. I've been wanting to try it…without penetration.

RONNIE: I could do that.

(RONNIE and SOPHIA go to his room.)

(Flip to MARCUS and CLARK's condo.)

MARCUS: How could I have lost control like that?

CLARK: I know—

MARCUS: It was like boiling oil just pouring out of me. And then I pointed a gun at her.

CLARK: Yeah, but just for a second.

MARCUS: C'mon! I pointed a gun at a human being, Clark. A gun!

CLARK: Look at it this way. Anyone who has ever pointed a gun at another person's face and then actually shot that person in the face would commend you on your restraint.

(MARCUS *exits to the kitchen.* CLARK *follows.*)

CLARK: I thought that was funny—

(RHONDA *enters from the kitchen, followed by* DONALD. *They're carrying casserole dishes full of food.*)

DONALD: You're not going over there.

RHONDA: What, Donald, what would Jesus do?

DONALD: He would not go over there!

RHONDA: I'm giving them the Pizza Spaghetti Casserole I prepped earlier

DONALD: They're not going to want our casserole—

RHONDA: All they'll have to do is bake it, Don!

DONALD: Oh, Rhonda—

RHONDA: —and what's left of this Green Bean Casserole. And all of the ingredients they'll need to make a taco ring. And I'll make them dinner every night for the rest of my life!

DONALD: He called you a racist and the—cunt word. Then he pointed a gun at you—

RHONDA: He didn't mean it. It was just society or whatever. Society was pointing that gun at me. It was Marcus that didn't pull the trigger.

DONALD: I'm not going.

RHONDA: Donald, we can bridge this gap we got here. Me and you. We can be the people that reach across— across the aisle and—and shake the hand of the gay blacks—um—the latinos, drug addicts, the college professors and people like that. We're good people. We're the best kind of people. We're Christian people, Donald. Everything that happened tonight can be fixed if we're just willing to talk to each other, admit mistakes and try to do better. We can do that.

DONALD: I don't know—

RHONDA: You know they're over there saying the exact same thing. I'm sure he's planning his apology right now—

(MARCUS *enters from the kitchen, followed by* CLARK.)

MARCUS: Fuck those fucking people! Seriously, Oh my god!

CLARK: A second ago you were all embarrassed about how angry you got—

MARCUS: Well, the anger's back. It's a circle of rage, Clark. Why don't you feel it? Aren't you angry?

CLARK: Well...

MARCUS: She called me a nigger.

CLARK: What did you expect? She likes White Zinfandel.

MARCUS: No, they're just—they're... I don't know, are they bad people?

CLARK: Yes! So don't worry so much about them.

MARCUS: Why do you want to sweep this under the rug?

CLARK: I don't—

MARCUS: And that whole scene, and you're relaxed and making jokes.

CLARK: I'm not relaxed. I'm having a panic attack.

He takes a drink. Pause.

MARCUS: Should you sit down?

CLARK: I believe I should. That's better. Is it possible to get more charming during a panic attack?

MARCUS: No.

CLARK: You know I know there are still people out there that want me dead because I'm gay. I think we all know that. Right? I choose to stay away from those people. That's why we live in this neighborhood; so we can walk down the street holding hands without fear. I just don't want you drawn into anything more... It's okay to write them off and move on.

(Blackout on MARCUS *and* CLARK. *Lights up on* RHONDA *and* DONALD.*)*

RHONDA: I wanna go over there. I do! I'm just so scared—

DONALD: He still has my gun—

RHONDA: Not of that, Don! I'm not scared of no gun. You're always saying guns don't kill people.

DONALD: But people with guns that you just called the N word might.

RHONDA: He's not going to shoot me. Still, I'm scared to face him after what I s—
(She cries.)

DONALD: Oh, Rhonda...

RHONDA: I'm just gonna go over there and I'm gonna give them our food and apologize.

DONALD: If you're fixin to go, I'm going with you.
(Pause)
Well...we going?

RHONDA: I'm trying to move my legs. I think they're scared.

(Black out on DONALD *and* RHONDA. *Lights up on* MARCUS *and* CLARK. *They go about clearing the dinner table.)*

CLARK: I'm agreeing with you!

MARCUS: —I'm just saying that you have no idea where—you obviously have no clue where I'm coming from—

CLARK: I've been discriminated against my entire life, too!

MARCUS: You're white!

CLARK: Yeah, but I'm gayer than you—

MARCUS: Gayer—

CLARK: You can pass! When I was seven years old my gym coach asked me if I liked U T or Oklahoma, and I was embarrassed I didn't know there was a musical called U T!

MARCUS: Yes, but, Clark I've lived with a quadr—

CLARK: —Quadruple consciousness—

MARCUS: —it's a thing—

CLARK: I'm not denying that—

(Their doorbell rings. MARCUS crosses to answer while still making his point.)

MARCUS: You sympathize but you can't empathize whether you're married to a black man or—

(MARCUS opens the door. RHONDA is there with DONALD behind her.)

RHONDA: Hi. I just wanted to—

(MARCUS shuts the door. The door bell rings again. And again. He gathers himself and opens the door.)

RHONDA: Hi, it's just us. Don't shoot us… That's a joke.

(Beat. MARCUS crosses to the couch and sits.)

MARCUS: Hilarious.

RHONDA: Don, dang it. Don, said I should start with a joke…to break the tension.
(Beat)
Anyhoo…I've brought a peace offering. This is—this is a casserole. We were gonna have it tomorrow. Pizza Spaghetti—

DONALD: It's good.

RHONDA: Pepperoni and Italian sausage and noodles and shredded mozzarella. Two jars of Prego. It's all made up. Just bake it at three hundred and fifty for an hour and it'll be ready to go. And this is half of a green bean casserole, it warms up good in the microwave. Just put a wet paper towel over it and zap it for two minutes. Well, our microwave is one of the big ones. Eleven hundred watts so, I didn't notice the size of yours so it might take more time. The casseroles are for the whole N word thing.

MARCUS: Thank you, Rhonda. I admire your guts at least.

DONALD: Great. Let's go—

RHONDA: Thank you.
(Pause)
Is there something you'd like to say to me?

MARCUS: Umm… Our microwave is nine hundred watts.

RHONDA: Good. Good. Might want to add a little time then… Did you want to apologize to me, too?

MARCUS: For…?

RHONDA: You…did call us white people.

MARCUS: Yes…and…?

RHONDA: You said it in a very mean way. With cuss words around it.

MARCUS: Yes. Would you like the rest of our mousse?

CLARK: Marcus. C'mon, now. They came over here to give us a bunch of very heavy foods.

MARCUS: I don't want to let them off the hook that easy—

RHONDA: You pointed a gun at me!

MARCUS: Barely!

RHONDA: You were very mean to us—

MARCUS: Donald made racially insensitive remarks all night long—

RHONDA: That's because he's stupid! Sorry, honey— He's really stupid when it comes to talking to people that he doesn't know anything about and he doesn't know anything about anybody. He doesn't have a racist bone in his body. You have to believe me. He's just has a bunch of stupid bones—

DONALD: Rhonda, damnit—

RHONDA: Can't you see how guilty I feel! Isn't that enough?!

MARCUS: Absolutely not. Those words were right there on the tip of your tongue—

RHONDA: I know—

MARCUS: Why do you think that is?

RHONDA: I've heard 'em a lot, Marcus. I grew up in East Texas in the fifties and people didn't just say it when they were mad. They said it every day.

DONALD: It's true—

RHONDA: My daddy named our old black dog the N-word.

CLARK: Jesus—

RHONDA: And that dog was always runnin' off. And so daddy was always having to stand out in the yard and yell for him. "Oh, N-word! Come home, N-word!" One time he didn't come home and so daddy and mama and all us kids went out through the neighborhood, all ten of us walking every street in town, hollering the N-word at the top of our lungs. And nobody thought nothing of it.

(Beat)

MARCUS: Well, that makes me feel better.

RHONDA: Good. Good! I'm glad, because it's true. So, can we be friends again?

MARCUS: That story doesn— We were never friends. Clark made me invite you over because he thought it would be funny. Something funny to joke about with our friends.

RHONDA: Is that true, Clark?

CLARK: No… Yes—but I feel guilty about it.

RHONDA: Oh, Clark.

CLARK: I'm sorry.

RHONDA: I thought we were getting on—

CLARK: We were. We were getting on right up until we weren't—

RHONDA: Then why?

CLARK: It was kinda like that movie—I can't remember the name. This guy and his buddies have a bet to see who can pick up the ugliest girl but the guy ends up liking the ugly girl he picks up.

RHONDA: I'm the ugly girl?

CLARK: Yes!

RHONDA: Oh, Clark!

CLARK: I'm trying to say I like you! Liked you! Until I didn't!

RHONDA: I thought you liked my hair. I know I'm old but I used to be pretty!

DONALD: She did! She used to be real pretty!

RHONDA: And—and—ya'll are just about the meanest, most impossible couple of folks I ever met!

CLARK: C'mon, Rhonda—

RHONDA: I'm a nice person! Don, tell them how upset I was at myself.

DONALD: She was pretty upset.

RHONDA: I'm sorry. I'm sorry, I'm sorry. I'm sorry, Marcus. Really.

CLARK: Marcus, just tell the woman you're sorry, too. Even if you don't mean it.

MARCUS: It—the whole thing is inexcusable. I can't explain to you what this is like. Words matter to me. They just do. Look, I know that I might have lost my temper, too, but.. It's just irreparable. I don't want your casserole.

RHONDA: Marcus, refusing a woman's casserole is the ultimate rejection.

DONALD: That's true.

RHONDA: I don't say that word. I said it but I don't say it!

MARCUS: You're the type of person, Rhonda, who hates certain types of people.

RHONDA: I do not!

CLARK: Oh, god. Come off it. Yes you do. But look, we all hate certain types of people.

MARCUS: You should be fully on my side here but you're defending them—

RHONDA: And we appreciate it.

CLARK: I'm not defending them! They do—You—You remind me of my parents. Who are dead—

RHONDA: Awwe—

CLARK: It's okay. I hated them. They never sat down to a meal with Marcus and me. Not one single meal.

They wrote us off. But you came over and—Look, wherever—however we got it, we all hold a certain amount of "hate"—fear or resentment—disgust—whatever—fear of certain types of people.

MARCUS: Not me.

CLARK: You hate people from Philadelphia.

MARCUS: Everybody hates people from Philadelphia!

DONALD: He's right about that.

CLARK: You hate ignorant, cloistered white people like Rhonda and Don.
(*To* RHONDA *and* DONALD)
Sorry, but, come on, everybody! A little more than half the country hates people like Rhonda and Don! Sorry. And about half hate us. I kind of get off on it.

MARCUS: Jesus.

CLARK: (*He starts rolling. Thinking out loud, connecting dots*) So, just— If you, Marcus. And you, Rhonda. And Donald. And me. If I could be honest. If we could share— Look, I know I'm just the funny, super lovable gay guy—a veritable quip machine. And I know that I joke around too much about this serious stuff and I've had a bottle of wine and maybe that's not that helpful in these situations but I think— Okay. I know the best and worst of Marcus. I love the best and I accept the worst because he's let me see it and admitted it's there…I mean he didn't show me his shit and try to convince me it was chocolate mousse because he knows I might eat it and he doesn't want me to eat—

MARCUS: Clark—

CLARK: —Right. But we didn't get to the trust we have without dropping a truth bomb or two or fifty over the last twenty five years. Telling the truth about the worst part of ourselves is just about the hardest thing in the world. I realize this whole racial and political divide in America is a big problem, but if you gimme a minute I think I can fix it.

MARCUS: Jesus.

CLARK: Now, I loved Rhonda's N-word dog story.

RHONDA: Oh, thank you.

CLARK: Well, yeah, that was—that was a real shameful piece of Americana, but you shared it and now I know a little more about where you're coming from. A terrible place. Those were not the good ol' days. And you ain't past it, girl. You are not as good of a person as you think you are. And I get that casseroles are your love language. All that together is one big 'ol truth bomb, Rhonda. Here's one about me. I use the phrase "Indian Giver" with impunity. Ah! Me! Married to a black man and I'm insensitive.

MARCUS: What are you doing?

DONALD: You can't say Indian Giver anymore?

MARCUS: No.

DONALD: Well, I'll be.

CLARK: Midgets freak me out.

RHONDA: Me too!

CLARK: I just can't deal with their little hands—

RHONDA: —Right!

CLARK: —but I know that's because I've never known one—

RHONDA: Yes!

CLARK: If I had a little—midget person in my life I'd probably fight like hell for them.

RHONDA: I'd probably take their little hands and help them over stuff.

CLARK: See!? We're becoming more tolerant already. Do you have a truth bomb you'd like to drop, baby?

MARCUS: I would honestly like to go to bed.

CLARK: Donald? Anything to get off your chest?

RHONDA: Good luck with him. That's a closed door.

CLARK: Not into sharing his feelings?

RHONDA: Feeling. He's not into sharing his feeling.

CLARK: Oh! Nice truth bomb.

MARCUS: Stop saying truth bomb. It's stupid.

CLARK: That was a truth bomb. Um, my turn again. Rhonda, when I was telling you about you reminding me of the gal that sang at the Hide Away…that's a drag bar…

RHONDA: Rachel Tension was a man?

CLARK: Rachel Tension was a man. And, as it turns out, a tidy bit of foreshadowing.

(On the other side of the stage, RONNIE sneaks out of his room and quietly looks around for DONALD and RHONDA.)

RHONDA: Oh. Okay.

CLARK: I feel unburdened. Who's next?

RHONDA: Our grand baby's face gives me the nightmares.

CLARK: Kaboom.

DONALD: Rhonda!

CLARK: Truth. Bomb.

RHONDA: I want to love her but…she looks like a spider.

CLARK: Wow. Wow. She does. She looks vaguely arachnid. Marcus, baby, do you not agree that it's important to admit this stuff about ourselves?

MARCUS: Why?

CLARK: I don't know! Do you not just seethe about a certain group of people?

Ronnie emerges from his room.

RONNIE: They're not here.

(SOPHIA *pokes her head out of the room.*)

MARCUS: No. I judge people as individuals only.

SOPHIA: Where do you think they went?

(*This action should overlap the following dialogue.* RONNIE *shrugs and disappears into the kitchen.* SOPHIA *sits on the couch and looks at her phone.*)

(RONNIE *enters from the kitchen with some Sunny D.* SOPHIA *has gotten out her headphones and a splitter.*)

SOPHIA: Headphones?

(RONNIE *goes into his room and gets some. Over the rest of the play they sit on the couch together listening to music that* SOPHIA *is sharing with him. They drink Sunny D.*)

CLARK: But, remember we thought it was so funny they were living in the gay neighborhood—I would do an impression of Donald under my breath when they saw us, "Uh, oh. They smiled at me. Now I got the AIDS."

RHONDA: That's not how you get the AIDS, Don!

CLARK: No, it was me putting that on him! But you're gay friendlier than that, right?

RHONDA: Absolutely! Right, Don!

DONALD: Right.

CLARK: (*To* MARCUS) See?!

DONALD: As long as you're not trying to recruit kids, it's none of our business.

CLARK: Jesus...

RHONDA: And I think you should be allowed to get married.

CLARK: We are allowed and we did!

RHONDA: Oh! Then congratulations!

CLARK: Thanks!

RHONDA: Yep, it's none of our business. I admit every time I picture you two being intimate it's not my cup of tea—

CLARK: Why are you picturing that?

RHONDA: I don't know!

CLARK: Well, stop. That fixes that!

DONALD: I had— Um…had two older brothers.

CLARK: Here we go.

DONALD: Adam was six years older than me and Luke was ten years older. Our daddy had died when I was pretty near a baby so Luke was the man of the house. I wanted to be just like them. They taught me to hunt and fight, and play ball, and swim. They were good brothers. But when I was twelve or thereabouts, one night they had me jump in Adam's pick up truck and off we went down to Rhekopffs, our little grocery store in town.

RHONDA: Right. Rhekopff's.

DONALD: Had a butcher and all the stuff you needed. They were closing up and we just sat out and waited. Out came Mr Rekopff and the old lady, Ms Velma, that ran the cash register and a black boy that was the—the stock boy, bag boy. The other two drove off and the black boy was on foot heading up to the hill—where all the black folks lived. Luke was driving and let him get a ways and then started the truck up and we followed him. My brothers weren't talking none. If I asked what we was doing they'd just shush

me. But I knew we were up to no good. Now, I didn't
know none of this at the time but apparently earlier
that week that black boy had said something uppity
to Mr Miles at Mr Miles' drugstore and Adam had
been in there to hear it. I don't know what it was, but
Adam had told Luke and Luke was…well, he set out
to teach that boy a lesson. So, we followed him a little,
slow, staying behind him. Then he started running.
Luke drove around him and pulled the truck around
in front of him. I thought we were going to run him
over. Then my brothers jumped out of the truck. Adam
caught ahold of him. The boy fought back but he was
real skinny…and between Adam and Luke they flung
him around like he was filled with hay. The boy was
yelling for help the whole time. I remember sitting in
the truck on my knees, looking through the window,
seeing Adam grab him and pull his head back. Luke
took two running steps and kicked that boy in the—the
head like it was a football. I could hear it through the
glass. The crunch. God. My brothers got back in the
truck, all out of breath, and excited and hoopin' and
hollerin', cussin'. We peeled outta there and just left
that boy to die. I was just sure he was dead. I was sure
I'd just watched my brothers kill a boy. He didn't die.
But he always had a dent in his head, or it—it wasn't
shaped right after. I would hide from him every time
mama'd take me into Rhekopff's but I got a good look
at him a few times. Besides his head being…different,
he seemed different, too. Looking at his shoes all the
time. Moved real slow.
I never loved my brothers again. I never saw them as
fun, big boys again. They looked like animals to me.
Like big, scary animals. I didn't know that boy but I
knew what they did made me so sick. They're dead
now. Adam died in a car wreck in 71. Luke died last
year. He got throat cancer from chewing his tobacco. I
didn't—I hadn't talked to either one of them for years

before they died. But I never—I never did tell anybody. I never told them what I thought. I was, just like that night, I was too chicken. I was too much of a chicken shit—I just never, once they were out of the house, I never went out of my way to talk to them. But— That's all I did. I didn't tell the police, I didn't tell our mama, I didn't look at their faces and say "shame on you". I didn't tell that poor boy with the crooked head what I'd seen and that I was sorry. I didn't do none of that.

(Pause)

CLARK: I eat Chic-Fil-A three times a week.

(They look at CLARK. *He's really broken up. Pause)*

RHONDA: *(To* DONALD*)* Who are you?

DONALD: I don't know.

MARCUS: I hate my brother, too. I hate him. He's… Growing up he was always superior to me. He was bigger and stronger and straight. He called me faggot more than he called me Marcus. Then he just failed. Over and over again. Got mixed up with that woman and, yes, drugs. He couldn't stay out of jail. Our parents worked so hard. We were middle class. And he chose that. I hated that. And he got to have a kid. I was doing everything right. I was making a future. I had love and was in graduate school. Making a real career. And he was able to have a kid. One night Clark and I got a call that she was in the E R. When the police went in, they were asleep, and she had pulled the television over on herself, her parents so high in the next room they couldn't be bothered to help that little baby. We took her home from the hospital and she's been ours ever since. How could he not have wanted what turned out to be the most important thing in my life? And she looks like him. Nothing like me. She looks just like him. My…one of my aunts, years ago, called me and said that he was clean, had been for years, was working at Wal-Mart, and he wanted to see her.

CLARK: What?

MARCUS: He wanted to be in her life. He'd heard so much and he was so proud. I said fuck no. She is my child. She's mine. Even if he is changed, I couldn't bear to see her with him. Even if it made her happy. Especially if it made her happy.

(Pause)

CLARK: That's probably enough truth bombs for one night, huh?

RHONDA: Yes. We should be going. I'm sorry about everything.

MARCUS: Hmm... Yeah—

RHONDA: You don't have to apologize.

MARCUS: I wasn't going to.

RHONDA: Okeedokee.

MARCUS: I don't think we're compatible. But we're neighbors. Can't change that. But I think—I just hope our pasts die with us, is all I'm saying.

RHONDA: Me too... Our pasts suck. Now, I want ya'll to keep those casseroles.

CLARK: Oh, I was planning on it, girl.

RHONDA: Three hundred and fifty degrees for an hour.

CLARK: Three hundred and fifty. Got it.

RHONDA: Just return the dishes and the server when you're done. No hurry.

CLARK: We know where to find you.

RHONDA: Well, come on, Don. Let's go home.

DONALD: Yep.

CLARK: Oh! I think the upside of all of this is that no one got shot.

(*He goes to get the gun.*)

RHONDA: Lord, I forgot about the gun.

CLARK: I wonder what Chekhov would say?

(*Beat. Confusion*)

CLARK: Oh, never mind.

(*The gun goes off and shoots* DONALD *in the upper thigh. The group exclaims.*)

DONALD: ARGGH!!!

RHONDA: Donald!

CLARK: Whoops!

MARCUS: What did you do?!

CLARK: It was an accident!

RHONDA: Oh! Don! Don!

CLARK: It just went off!

DONALD: My leg. Oh, god. I think—argghh—

RHONDA: Be still, Don. Oh, oh! What do we do! What do we do!?

DONALD: Oh, god!

CLARK: Is it his penis?

MARCUS: Clark, Call 911. It's okay. It's not his penis.

DONALD: Thank god.

CLARK: Thank god.

MARCUS: It's your upper thigh, Don.
(*He tears off his shirt.*)
Don, I bet this will hurt.

(MARCUS *presses the shirt to* DONALD's *wound. It hurts.*)

CLARK: Hello!? Is this 911? A man has been shot in my apartment. 3857—

DONALD: Ahh!

CLARK: —3857 Cedar Springs. Apartment 2D—

MARCUS: Rhonda, get me your serving spoon over there. Clark, give me your braided belt—

(CLARK *takes his belt off.*)

CLARK: Yes. We were having a perfectly lovely dinner party then the gun came out and yada yada yada I accidentally shot him in the leg.

MARCUS: Let's get him to the couch for this.

RHONDA: But— Your couch! It's ecru!

MARCUS: Rhonda!

RHONDA: Right—Stay right there.

(RHONDA *runs next door to her apartment and disappears down the hall, then sprints out with their shower curtain with the rings still attached.* RONNIE *and* SOPHIA *don't see her but look at each other when she slams the door. She bursts back into the other apartment and puts the shower curtain over the couch to protect it from blood.*)

MARCUS: Okay…

(RHONDA *helps* MARCUS *get* DONALD *to the couch and starts working on making the serving spoon and the belt into a tourniquet.*)

CLARK: Yes. He's in pain but he's awake. My husband is trying to stop the bleeding.

MARCUS: Ready, Don?

DONALD: Yep.

(MARCUS *twists the spoon, tightening the tourniquet and* DONALD *screams.*)

RHONDA: Oh, Don!

CLARK: Oh, Jesus. Now, this is real important so listen and write it down, type it down. He was accidentally shot by me. Clark Coleman. Matthew Clark Coleman.

MARCUS: Okay?

DONALD: Yeah.

CLARK: I am white, wearing a purple shirt, chestnut hair. Please tell the police that there is a shirtless black man in the room but he did not do anything. It was me. Matthew Clark Coleman. Type it down.

MARCUS: I'm going to elevate your leg—

CLARK: No, just—just tell the police people that are coming that it was the white guy in the purple shirt. Hmm? Chestnut. Like, a light brown. Yes. The black guy with his shirt off who is sort of hovering over the victim didn't do anything. Yes, shirtless. Okay? Thank you, honey. Yes. I'll—I'll stay on the line... They're coming.

MARCUS: Okay. Hold tight.

DONALD: I wanna say something—

MARCUS: Save your energy.

DONALD: I got another one of them truth bombs. I've always fantasized...

MARCUS: Oh, no...

DONALD: I've always daydreamed about having a black friend. I picture us watching T V together, like Twelve Years a Slave or Roots, something he'd like...

MARCUS: Oh, God—

DONALD: And he'd know I wasn't a bad guy at heart and I'd know he was a nice guy and we'd know each other's families and we'd have a hand shake we'd do every time we saw each other. Something kind of elaborate. And we'd be friends. Like me and a nice black guy. Not a gangstery or, or hip hoppy type of guy. Just a nice black guy. Anyway… That's just something I've always thought about. Maybe it was guilt from what my brothers did or, I don't know… maybe it was ever since I saw Stir Crazy. Maybe I could learn something from him. I don't know.

(Pause. MARCUS shakes his head, looks to the heavens for strength, takes a breath, and offers DON his hand. They fumble through a handshake.)

MARCUS: Okay. You relax. They'll be here any minute.

(RHONDA puts her hand on MARCUS and CLARK's shoulders.)

RHONDA: It's just like Mr Rogers said.

(They all look at RHONDA. Then they all wait. The lights fade on them.)

(SOPHIA gets RONNIE's attention.)

SOPHIA: We should get some pizza.

RONNIE: Huh. Yeah. Oh, yeah.

SOPHIA: Coo. What do you want?

RONNIE: Hawaiian?

SOPHIA: Pineapple? On a pizza? Nigga please. I like plain cheese.

RONNIE: Cheese pizza is gay.

(The lights fade on RONNIE and SOPHIA.)

END OF PLAY

CPSIA information can be obtained
at www.ICGtesting.com
Printed in the USA
BVHW042110300120
571034BV00008B/127